BEI GRIN MACHT SICH IHR
WISSEN BEZAHLT

- Wir veröffentlichen Ihre Hausarbeit,
  Bachelor- und Masterarbeit

- Ihr eigenes eBook und Buch -
  weltweit in allen wichtigen Shops

- Verdienen Sie an jedem Verkauf

Jetzt bei www.GRIN.com hochladen
und kostenlos publizieren

Mishel Marcus

Judith as a trickster or Judith as a cleric?

Book of Judith, Old Testament of the Bible

GRIN Verlag

Bibliografische Information der Deutschen Nationalbibliothek:

Die Deutsche Bibliothek verzeichnet diese Publikation in der Deutschen National-
bibliografie; detaillierte bibliografische Daten sind im Internet über http://dnb.d-
nb.de/ abrufbar.

Impressum:

Copyright © 2013 GRIN Verlag GmbH
Druck und Bindung: Books on Demand GmbH, Norderstedt Germany
ISBN: 978-3-656-60666-6

Dieses Buch bei GRIN:

http://www.grin.com/de/e-book/269515/judith-as-a-trickster-or-judith-as-a-cleric

Individual Research Report

The Book of Judith is part of the Old Testament of the Bible. In contrast to other books of the Bible, the story is wholly fictional and just composed in order to outline the history of the Israeli throughout the previous 400 years. The book is written in the second or third century before Christ and is divided into 16 chapters. The story deals with Judith, a pious widow who is able to defeat Holofernes, who besieged her town Bethulia. Holofernes, a general under the Assyrian king Nebuchadnezzar was ordered to conquer and punish all countries which did not help him in his campaign against the Meder. As all countries in Asia Minor and Syria were conquered, the army reached Bethulia which they besieged as it was the only city which did not surrender. Despite the fact that the inhabitants of Bethulia gave up hope, Judith was the only one who relied on God. She left the besieged city and went down to Holofernes's camp where she pretended to be a defector. Blinded by her beauty and her wisdom, Holofernes allowed her access to his tent where Judith used her chance and decapitated him as he was sleeping drunk in his bed. With this action she saved her town and the Israeli.

The Book of Judith therefore tells us a story of a woman who is able to kill a mighty warrior on her own only with the help of God on whom she relied. Judith's image has gone through many changes throughout the history which differs from a pious theologian to a trickster. In the following, I am going to analyze these images in order to contrast them. My aim is to find out which image suits better: Judith as a trickster or Judith as a cleric?

Already in the medieval times, different views of Judith existed as those were largely a result of ideas in poems brought up by different authors. On the one hand, she was praised for her chastity and her refusal to dishonor her body with impure beverage and food (Estes 326). On the other hand, there was also a different view of Judith: Judith as a trickster which only was able to defeat Holofernes with the help of her stunning beauty (ibid. 327-328).

First of all, I am going to start with the trickster image of Judith. She is described as "[...] very beautiful, charming to see" (Jdt 8,7) but this is also connected with a moral degradation as beauty is equated with evilness and furtiveness. This can also be found in the story itself

1

where she kills Holofernes but also in her speech to Holofernes where she succeed in persuading Holofernes to wait for her signal when to attack Bethulia as she would know if the Israeli would sin against their God. Holofernes is seduced by her speech but even more stunned by her beauty. If you take a closer look at the speech, you will see that Judith uses several techniques to achieve her aim. First of all, she flatters Holofernes by saying that the Israeli "[…] have indeed heard of [his] genius and adroitness of mind" (Jdt 11,11) with which she states that Holofernes genius was announced in the whole world and that he exceeded other generals (Schmitz 335). The second technique she uses is irony. She implies ambiguities in her speech, e.g. when she promises that Holofernes will be successful in Judaea.

I shall be your guide right across Judea until you reach Jerusalem; there I shall enthrone you in the very middle of the city. And then you can round them up like shepherd-less sheep, with never a dog daring to bark at you. Foreknowledge tells me this; this had been foretold to me and I have been sent to reveal it to you (Jdt 11,19).

This happens also in the story but not in the way like Holofernes believed. His soil is donated to the temple of Jerusalem (Jdt 16,19). One can see that Judith's success was only possible with her cheating and use of irony which justifies the term trickster.

Apart from this trickster motive, there is the image of Judith as a cleric. She is described as a person who knows a lot about her religion and God's plan which allows her to carry out her plan successfully. There are several passages which strengthens this claim. The first passage can be found in the 8th chapter where Judith reminds the elders that they made a wrong decision by reminding them the example of the patriarchs Abraham, Isaac and Jacob. Furthermore, Judith begs for God's help before she goes out to defeat Holofernes. Her voluntary nudeness during her prayer can be seen as an act of self-humiliation with which she points out the danger of a possible violation (Schmitz 224). Judith prays in the position of a self surrender where she undergoes her possible destiny of rape (ibid. 225). She cries out for God's help who is described as a savior of the poor and humble. From this point she turns out from a pious and rich widow to a beautiful woman (ibid.). Another striking point is the repetition of the hand motive which appears 19 times throughout the story. There is a slight difference; on the one hand she is the one who kills Holofernes with her own hands but on the other hand it is emphasized that God killed Holofernes through her hands. (ibid. 406). Nevertheless, Judith can also be seen as a new Moses who recognizes God's signs and knows how to act in the following.

As we can see, Judith images as trickster or as theologian do not exclude each other but on the contrary, are referred to each other. On the one hand she is a trickster who is able to defeat her enemy with her beauty. On the other hand she is a theologian, the only one who is able to read God's sign and to act accordingly. Nevertheless, these two images are connected. Judith's beauty is an expression of her wisdom and her fear of God. She only uses her beauty and the seduction connected with it to save her fellow men and to save Israel from the heathen.

During my individual research I gained a profound insight into the Book of Judith. I would never have thought that the story of Judith was full of symbols and references to other stories in the Bible. It was interesting to see which methods Judith used to achieve her aim. I must admit that the research report was quite challenging because I did not know on which aspect I should have put the focus. During the reading of the Book of Judith, I found out that Judith was characterized with the two different images so that I decided to compare these images to find out why the author of the book used those. As a conclusion, I can say that this research report showed me that if one look closer into a text, one can gain new information one would never have thought of it.

Work Cited

Estes, Heide. "Feasting with Holofernes: Digesting Judith in Anglo-Saxon England." *Exemplaria* 15 (2003): 325-350.

Schmitz, Barbara. *Gedeutete Geschichte. Die Funktion der Reden und Gebete im Buch Judit.* Freiburg: Herder 2004.

Schmitz Barbara. „Trickster, Schriftgelehrte oder femme fatale? Die Juditfigur zwischen biblischer Erzählung und kunstgeschichtlicher Rezeption." *Biblisches Forum* (2004): 1-16.

"Book of Judith." New Jerusalem Bible. 17 July 2013 <http://www.catholic.org/bible/book.php?id=18>.